A FAREWELL SERMON

DELIVERED IN THE

First Presbyterian Church

Ann Arbor, Michigan

BY

REV. SAMUEL W. DUFFIELD

SUNDAY EVENING, NOV. 29, 1874.

PUBLISHED BY REQUEST.

ANN ARBOR
COURIER STEAM PRINTING HOUSE
1874

To the

Church and Congregation

who have joined

with me

in Labor and in Prayer

I Dedicate

this

our united story

of Struggle and Success

Samuel W. Duffield.

Dec. 1, 1874.

CIVITAS DEI.

"For my brethren and companions' sakes I will now say,
Peace be within thee!"

City of God, grown old with silent faces
Lying beneath the shadow of the clay,
Thine are the towers built up in barren places,
Thine the great bastions waiting for the day.

Dim through the night stone after stone arises,
Bold through the dawn step forth the peaks of flame,
Touched with the splendor of those glad surprises
By which the blessing of the Spirit came.

Toilers of truth are we, who at our labor
Keep the sharp sword still girded at the thigh,
Heeding no summons of the pipe and tabor,
Fighting and building till the end be nigh.

. . . .

Thus, then, we build through storm and pleasant weather;
Thus, then, we pray by morning and by night;
Heart knit with heart, and hands at work together—
Beset by foes until Thou givest light.

City of God! thy peace is our petition;
City of God! our brethren dwell in thee;
And for their sakes, in true and deep contrition,
We seek thy good, O dwelling of the free.

S. W. D.

From "Warp and Woof" (1870).

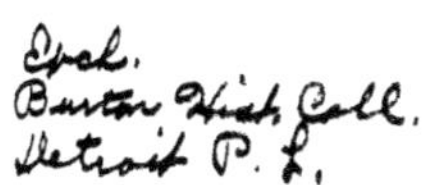

A FAREWELL SERMON.

"These things have I told you, that when the time shall come ye may remember that I told you of them. And these things I said not unto you at the beginning, because I was with you."—JOHN xvi. 4.

THE loveliest evening often succeeds the stormiest day. An obscured sun, hidden through many hours by mists and vapors, has at length shown for a moment the brightness of its light. Far peaks glow in a level splendor which stays for no descent into the vale between. The distant ocean shines in the new and unexpected glory. And you and I, pilgrims and strangers, rejoice in the coming and lament at the going of that sunny ray which

"Smote the white sails of ships that wore
Outward or in, and gilded o'er
The steeples with their veering vanes."

Thus it must have been in the earthly history of our Lord and Saviour Jesus Christ. Hidden by the veil—"that is to say, His flesh"—the true divinity of light was seldom seen. The rays which here and there appeared, were thought by most to be but reflections or scintillations from a pure character and a noble heart. That this carpenter's son could be God's son, was hard to comprehend. And every error which has since prevailed respecting the person and work of Christ, finds its origin in this short-sighted judgment "after the outward appearance." Seldom did He declare Himself in actual words. A Samaritan woman of no reputation, a Jewish ruler of the temple conversing with Him at dead of night, a poor impulsive disciple—such as these heard Him announce His true Messiahship. To the wise and the learned and the rich—then as now—the face was a hidden face.

But when the near approach of death renders it fittest for Him to speak, we have the sunburst and the splendor. Compressed within a few short pages of a single Gospel, we find those "thoughts which breathe and words which burn," by which henceforth we may interpret the universe of God. The far-off summits of the truth are touched from this horizon, and the great deep of human wisdom becomes as brilliant as the ocean of Apocalypse.

And amid all this—just as He had revealed the immense possibilities of His character—He was to "go away." He was to leave the conversion of mankind to a few poor fishermen, a couple of publicans, a woman saved from seven devils, and such other feeble and insignificant folk as had followed Him out upon the road to Bethany, to watch Him vanish, like a vision, within the morning cloud. If there was grief because He left them, there was greater grief because of what was left behind.

Yet He had told them, in essence if not in substance, that after the night would come the morning—that this sunset of His person would be succeeded by the dawn of His Spirit. He asked only of them truth and trust, until the trial should be ended and the cloven flame should play about their heads. He might have prophesied that

"The new day comes, the light
Dearer for night."

But it would seem that in this, as in almost every event of His life, He transcended or reversed our human judgment. He points them not to the time to come so much as to the *securing* of that time —not so much to glory beyond, as to that tribulation and that persecution which made the glory sure. The light upon the peak gave a lustre even to the low valley.

Better than the wonderful story which the marvelous tinker fashioned in Bedford jail, is the record of this life and this departure—the Progress of the best of Pilgrims back unto His Father's house. And it is no forced or strained attempt for us to be so involved in His personality, through all His way in the world, that we too seem, as it were, to be treading in His steps and "filling up what is behind of the sufferings of Christ, for His body's sake, which is the church." To *this* that "Follow me!" calls us as well as them; and the occasions and circumstances—the trials and temptations and tears and pain—of our own existence, can be found interpreted in His.

Even our partings come beneath the same surpassing pattern. For if we are truly making God's will our rule, and if the word of His commandment is on "fleshly tables of the heart" which beats within our bosoms, we too may discover that "all things work for good," and that the methods of the "Most High" are, like His guiding light, invariable and without shadow of turning. And even as we now perceive that a deeper blessing followed because of the Christ who was parted from them—so each "good gift" and each "perfect gift" which we enjoy and which is taken from us, but brings a better in its place. Yet we all hold with tremulous fingers to the health or the hope or the home or the loved and dear ones, as God removes us from them and them from us. We should otherwise sin with lip and heart, and not knowing that which was for our highest profit we should simply rest and be at ease. Yet He who makes man's labor for his mouth to be the basis of all political economy, inspires in the soul that loves Him a like hunger, not to be appeased until the beatitude is complete, that "they who hunger and thirst after righteousness * * shall be filled."

Not impiously, then, nor from any endeavor to compare small things with great, do I point you in these, the closing services of an eventful pastorate, to the language of our Lord. If the true pastor be in the stead of the visible Christ, that he may illustrate by precept and example that attractive yet unparalleled life, it follows that he must "have the Spirit of Christ or he is none of His." Born again into a regeneration which leaves no room for self-seeking and no moment for repose, he can be at best but "a pilgrim and a stranger" tarrying over-night, a soldier "fighting the good fight of faith," a herald at the entrance of the stadium, watchful "lest he himself should be a castaway." The lessons of self-dependence we learn in almost every matter better than in religion. We strangely forget that in this, preëminently, our souls must seek the wisdom which is from above, and that we must, with all our love for the brethren, be individual inquirers after that will of God affecting *us* which is our highest rule of duty.

Absence has its advantages. It appears to have done everything for Peter and John—it certainly produced Stephen, and as certainly accomplished the divine decree. And, in every sundering of human relations, it bids us remember that "the whole family in heaven and on earth" are named by one name and are laboring in one love.

I. Three years ago I came among you "because thereto I was sent." It was certainly no cheerful prospect. Here stood a great unfinished church, with the nail-heads in their naked ugliness and the walls of the audience-room orange-tawny and indescribably depressing to the sight. A cold breeze plunged down upon the head of the preacher, and a mocking echo wandered and played in the angles of the bare and abandoned ceiling. Some of you sat upon your own purchased cushions, and many of you had nothing but the plain pine boards. As the church stood it was evidently the result of a good brave purpose, but debt had arisen and debt must be discharged. This irksome task fell upon my predecessor, and before it was fully rounded out, he, like others, had been overwhelmed by the weight he was to carry, and had no longer the heart to bear the load. Nor was it strange that he should feel as he did.

The disadvantages were thus very great. A prejudice had somehow sprung up—a thing which I now comprehend more clearly than I comprehended it then—and the church was almost deserted by the students of the University. Its important situation as the only church of our denomination by the side of a large and unsectarian institution of learning, had not been grasped thoroughly by either Presbytery or Synod. Financially it represented no great amount of capital. Mentally it had enormous demands. Spiritually it required patient and careful training, that the strong and contemplative piety of individual Christians might be all brought into one common purpose and turned toward active work. Socially it was charged with coldness, formality, and a predisposition to run into cliques and feuds.

On the contrary, the troublesome debt had been really paid. The building, so far as it went—truncated tower, paintless stairways, unadorned lecture-room, and fenceless grounds—was, notwithstanding, a most solid and admirable structure. There had been a revival, even in the *interregnum*, and some forty young people, mostly baptized children of the church, had been received. The necessity itself had obliterated many old marks of division, and had developed a fervent spirit of prayer for God's guidance. The Presbytery had offered special petitions to this same effect.

And I, myself, hurried by the Spirit, like Philip, into the way toward Gaza "which is desert," felt that He who had brought me hither could "make the wilderness to blossom as the rose."

II. The very first thing to be done was to secure the blessing of the great Head of the Church, by giving to Him and to the communion of His body and blood, the chief and foremost place. We first met at that dear Table, and there we have this day parted, and we have found no sweeter or more solemn pleasure than in commemorating His dying love. It was here that we learned to know each other's faith. It was here that we were renewed by bread from heaven, and found that the blood of Christ was life unto our souls. For I have endeavored to cause this ordinance to be to all of us just what, in simplicity and earnestness, a plain honest student of God's book perceives it to have been in the mind of Christ. Theology has never intruded here, to snatch from our lips the cup or to take from our hands the bread. Art and poetry, and the noblest and highest matters, have here, in this atmosphere of heart-life and perfect consecration, found their dearest home. And how often you have come to me, and with wet eyes gazing into wet eyes and hand warmly clasping hand, you have spoken of this joyfulness and blessing, you yourselves know full well. We have often been on the Hill called Clear, nay even we have walked and talked, beholding the golden streets of the New Jerusalem from Beulah Land itself.

Thus, with this consecration of our entire morning service, once in two months, to this happiest of all privileges, we began to find God's blessing among us. We began to pause after prayer-meeting, and to shake hands. Gradually the quiet and unobtrusive praying ones made themselves known. And on the principle that "he that believeth shall not make haste," I preferred rather to follow God's guidance than to anticipate it—but I dreaded that I might lag behind the purpose of Providence by so little as a single hour.

The need for change in the very *atmosphere* of the house and worship of God, cried out for attention and energy at the start. But to change an atmosphere requires a change in surroundings. And "surroundings," to begin with, meant new cushions and something more after the fashion of a pulpit than the existing structure on that wide waste of platform, over which those curious lanceolate pieces of wood gazed so benignantly into space. To those ladies who then and since have been identified with every good word and work, must be given the praise for our present most comfortable seats.

The pulpit has its own peculiarities. It aims to offend neither the lover of the old-time desk, nor the advocate of the new-time lectern. And yet it is no compromise. And it bears in unmistakeable characters its true commission, which is to "Preach the Word." Now and then I have thought that this pulpit, and this platform, are symbolic of those principles, upon which the preaching of these three years has been based. It has been both free and firm, and first of all, it has been fixed upon the Lord Jesus Christ. Behind this desk have

stood those brethren from abroad—whatsoever their creed--who have loved Him first and chief. Baptist and Congregationalist and Methodist and Presbyterian, high-church Lutheran and "broad-church" Church of England—all, in these three years, have had their representatives, and all have felt at home. And we never listened to words of more singular purity, originality, or devout Christliness, than those which fell from the lips of George MacDonald.

Yet this portion of the work was only premonitory. For, presently—with your good help and encouragement—we set about the reconstruction of the audience-room and building. It did not "rise into towers," mist-like, in the manner of fabled Ilium, but it rose into one tower which had never been before. It gathered its galleries about it, ribbed its ceiling with appropriate and architectural woods, and took on that new and bright appearance which every visitor so readily commends. Thanks to one generous heart, the "fair colors" of the walls and ceiling are also here, and will remain "in memorial of her" for many years to come. Presently a band of young ladies made it possible to "praise God with the organ," and a mighty bell took its place in the finished tower, and on it was inscribed:

> "Ring out the darkness of the land,
> Ring in the Christ that is to be!"

After a summer of most unclerical attitudes upon scaffolds higher than Haman's, the work for which we had so long waited was mainly complete; and at a cost far less than one could have supposed possible we were in possession of a beautiful and home-like audience-room. Paint and varnish had done their duty, and the prayer with which we began our labor had been answered, for amid all the dangers incident to many portions of the task, no accident of consequence had happened. There were narrow escapes, but there was no real injury. We could look upon it with gladness and thankfulness of heart, and pronounce it "very good." The poor man is not awed by its magnificence; the rich man cannot criticise its poverty; the man of taste cannot recoil from its incongruities; and last and best of all, the spiritual worshiper finds within it the air of home, of heart-life and of heaven. It has done more for us than anything besides the pure gospel.

Following this came the next summer's work upon lecture-room and grounds. The same atmosphere crept across them both, and if to no other care I could trust it, I think I might safely ask of our

thrifty ivies that they should keep my memory green. And thus, quietly and steadily, we took our station as a power for the truth in this city.

It may even now surprise you to be told that this reconstruction was so utter and absolute that it involved new articles of association, a new method in finance, and a new organization in many ways. But so it was.

III. In considering this steady line of progress, it is at once evident as being the result of deliberate and careful purpose; but no purpose, however deliberate and careful, could have succeeded unless by the blessing of God and the aid of the church. The prayers of Presbytery and Synod have been, at one time and another, specially offered for us. It may, therefore, be wise and well to disclose before you, not those matters which you accepted and supported as they were each announced, but the connection of one with the other in the long chain of events. For the spiritual and mental history are equally the result of God's guiding hand, and the relation of this church to great and grave questions of principle and policy should be by no means questionable.

1. When the providence of God called me to meet the rum-seller at the coffin of his victim, it was high time to speak of Temperance, and I endeavored to conceal nothing of the counsel of God against this curse. Then and since, the trumpet has given no uncertain sound.

When the demand of blatant sciolists came like the challenge of Goliath of Gath across the plain, we went against them with sword and spear, but we much preferred at length no armor of Saul—only the smooth stone from

> "Siloa's brook that flowed
> Fast by the oracle of God."

And we are pretty generally convinced that while science and skepticism must receive attention, and true science and honest doubt deserve even more than attention, the best assault upon their ranks is not made from their low level. To rise above, to better and purer air—to breathe a strength which is not in the place of battle—to *know* science and to *appreciate* doubt, but to soar, singing, beyond them all into the eye of the day—this is the more permanently powerful work. As some look upon this method, it becomes but the subterfuge of ignorance calling for "implicit faith" as against reason. But as *we* apprehend it, it proclaims faith to be the highest reason, intellect to be inferior to heart, confidence in God to be the surest road to knowledge, and Christ Jesus to be that wisdom before which this lower learning pales and fades, as the morning star before the sun. It cannot be charged upon the teachings of this pulpit, in these three years, that they have repressed thought, repelled inquiry, or disdained a state of "honest doubt." For we have believed that there are, in this community, many such uncertain, dubious minds, ill at ease, and seeking after rest within the truth. And we have even preferred their partial faith, to the thoughtless acquiescence in an unknown and unintelligible creed.

To all such, simple or subtle, we have as a church—in our public services, in our social and cottage meetings, and in our search of "wit, eloquence and poesy" in the Young People's Association—held up only Him who

> "Was nailed
> For our advantage on the bitter cross."

We have found no convincing argument so good as Christ Himself.

2. Aside from these public questions which from the state of the public mind must be as publicly met and moved, there have been other relations of vital value to us as a Society. We are associated with other evangelical churcnes in common labor for the common weal. We have found that by respecting our own rights and the rights of others, and by sincere and unsectarian desire for the salvation of souls, we were walking most nearly in the way of Christ. "As much as in us lay" we have "lived peaceably with all" who were of "the household of faith." May the day be far distant, when word or act of this church shall either surrender a single principle of importance to permanent Christian union. or consent to a false or factitious semblance, in the stead of that reality which now so generally exists!

3. Nor have we been able to overlook another duty—that, namely, to our own young people and, by example, to the young people of other churches. It took a considerable time before the way was clear for the organization of our Young Peoples' Association. But now it is a factor of the utmost consequence in the future of the church. Socially, intellectually, and in the matter of Christian training and aggressive work, it satisfies a want long felt in this peculiar field between the Church and the University. Here, on some sort of common ground, it is possible for us to meet all worthy and earnest young

people, and to make a strong link between the "stranger within our gates" and those who dwell at home. A literary element has been found of admirable service as a cohesive force, and the Sunday evening and Cottage prayer-meetings are religious centres. It is by the Cottage meetings more especially that the fire of real Christian sympathy and experience is borne from home to home, and from heart to heart.

4. To an exterior view there is one relation of this church which is anomalous, and which demands thorough consideration. It is its position beside the University of Michigan.

Were this Institution denominational, any attempt on the part of those who were of a different faith and order, to affect or influence students in a religious point of view, would be a decided impertinence. Had it an organized Church within its walls, it would be unjust and unfair to compete with its religious design. Did it make Protestant Christianity a fundamental article in its method of education, it would deserve and extend a wide charity. But it happens to be a State Institution in which no religious tests inhere, whose students are under no personal religious supervision, whose morning-prayers are strictly voluntary, and whose occasional religious efforts depend for their success upon their nature, season and promoters. That a religious feeling prevails at all within its halls and class-rooms, can be directly ascribed to the personal high character of some of its instructors, and to the presence of a Students' Christian Association, which, through negation and chill and discouragement, has seen its work crowned, during the last winter, with an abundant revival of the power of the Holy Ghost.

When I happened once to make a public statement of these patent facts, I found myself drawn back from the columns of a religious journal into the columns of the daily press. To your disgust, and my own, the issue of fact was forced upon me, and I have seen reason to hope that Christian people penetrated, even in that short contest, behind the fallacious comparisons of present with past. The exact state of religion in the University was reached in a single answer to a single question, asked by one of the famous committee who came to carry through that which they felt to be a solemn farce, and to inquire into "Sectarian instruction in religion and medicine." The question was put: "Does the University teach religion?" and the answer was given, "*Negatively*, yes." Which, if it means anything, can be logically construed as "*Affirmatively*, No!" And it is to be noticed that neither creed nor sect was comprehended in the query.

Was it, therefore, a misconception of the duty of this Church that it owed its service to those thus cast upon it? Do we differ in our feelings from the other churches of the city, when we include this as one of the main things to be reached in our work? Or should I have paid no attention to this mass of Twelve Hundred young men and women, simply culling out the Presbyterians, and holding forth no hand of welcome, and saying no word of aid to any of the rest? The attendance upon this congregation for the past two years, and the souls who have been saved, and the delight which has filled your own hearts prove the contrary.

Intangibilities are dangerous foes. To fight them is to fight "as one that beateth the air." But real and evident things are worthy of remark. Hence, called out by a desire for facts upon a given question, a word of mine spoken under the elms of Yale, and merely expressing a doubt as to the physical fitness of ladies for masculine study, was caught up and went echoing backward and forward through the land. But it encouraged me when I found, in the space of a fortnight after, that Professor Seelye, of Amherst, and Dr. Bellows, of New York, and presently, Dr. Clark, of Boston, placed their fingers on the same weak spot, and for the sake of all concerned called attention to it as I had done.

And I would be untrue to my own sense of honor, ungrateful to my remembrance of personal friendship, and dull and dead to any appreciation of deep Christianity, pure and noble lives, and high and successful endeavor, if I did not pay the tribute of sincere esteem to the womanly women of this University. That which I feared for them has been happily averted, and the future story of the Day of God will reveal that with Woman came into the University of Michigan heart, taste and a religious and social element of inexpressible importance.

In the midst of these strivings for the light, there was an unaccountable lack of cordial assistance on the part of the University authorities. Many saw it, some felt it, and some—though they were few in number—agonized over it. When, therefore, to the complete dismay of those who were nearest to the Christian heart of that institution, we were publicly informed that there was "no sympathy with this anxious solicitude" as to some of the present tendencies of Higher Education, and that this "transition-period" of student-life was to be left to run its course of skepticism that it might end in faith, it certainly claimed and obtained a reply. All the warnings and predictions of the Evangelical Alliance as to these tendencies revived at once, because the evidence was on the ground, and the effects were present before our eyes. Thus, the case at length demanded, and your pastor used "great plainness of speech," "without partiality and without hypocrisy."

Was it because of an unanswering God that *from that very night*, the Spirit of all Truth was striving among those students? Was it an unconscious comment on a certain proud carelessness for the souls beneath their charge, that the great blast bowed certain members of the Faculty, as it swept down the skeptic, and gave breath of life to many a fainting soul?

Since then the old struggle renews itself in another form. Could there be between these churches and the authorities of that institution, the friendship and fellowship which now prevail between us and our student-friends, it would indeed be a happy thing. These faithful, earnest students, whose zeal gives to the University the best of its repute, would be educated, not merely technically, but in the love of a broad, sweet culture, wrought through the spirit of Him of Nazareth, who "spake as never man spake" before or since.

Yet it is a main part of the intense difficulty, and the source of the most wearing anxiety of the pastorate in this church of ours, that this is emphatically *not* so. And the latter will forever kill—in religion and in learning—for the spirit alone giveth life.

Unsectarian, as it professes to be, there is no outlook for a permanent constituency to the University, except in some way through religious influence. And to place any denomination evidently in power, or to place any denomination evidently under the ban, is to cast off the sympathy and support of a certain constituency of evangelical christians.

You may remember that Prof. De Volson Wood served us in the Session and in the Board of Trustees, most admirably well. His department in the University gave it and him renown. But when he left —and his printed report makes plain why he did leave—we lost the only professor in the Literary Department who was identified with us. Our work has, hence, been very trying and perplexing. We ran the risk of appearing to intrude in every move we made; but it seemed clear that we must do our full duty, and leave the rest to God. I do not disguise from you, that in all ordinary expectation of justice, the

vacant place thus left in our working force should have been soon supplied. I refrain from criticism, but I cannot sufficiently express my regret that many should have been driven to believe that disinclination and not inability, operated against us. A consciousness of this fact has largely produced my consent to labor where I shall have, I trust, the same success without encountering forever the effect of whispers, hints, detractions, and whatever else might seek to nullify your success as well as mine. That this is no fancy, I am very sure. I have too frequent confirmation of the belief that this church, as it stands to-day in all its methods, arrangements and prosperity, is to be left to fight its battle alone for the souls of these young men and women, for me to be in doubt. I have been compelled, now and then, to step in advance of you and to take a position to which, very soon, I have secured your full consent. Once more, and for the last time, and in the presence of the Searcher of all hearts, I take before you the position that if you believe with the heart, if you love with the heart, if you go forward on your chosen path and do your chosen work, all will be well. This path may cross other paths, but there will be no collision. And if you do not share in a positive misconception of plan and labor, you shall be set free, finally, from a necessity for change which comes to whatever will not base itself upon the heart instead of the head. That this change is imminent in all education and in all religion, I have no fraction of doubt. Wisdom, whether in Christianity or in the integral calculus, is the product of a love for principles which transcends both creed and rule, useful and even necessary as they both must ever be. On this high plane you are now proceeding. Go forward upon it without let or hindrance, undismayed!

IV. This constitutes the outlook of your future work. This institution, wisely planned at the first by Christian men, shall endure undoubtedly to commemorate their christian zeal. But it may be permitted to a descendant of one of those earliest regents, to announce that the University as a fact is greater than any man, yea, than any administration or the policy of any administration. It can never remain the football of a faction, or the bema of a demagogue. Surely and steadily it will crystallize into a clear policy. The insects in the coral may perish, but the work shall live. Education is no deluded goddess—her name is rather to be called Wisdom.

> "Her open eyes desire the truth,
> The wisdom of a thousand years
> Is in them; may perpetual youth
> Keep bright their light from tears!"

Religion and Learning should be hand in hand. It is for you—in your sphere, and within the true limits of your own demesne—to keep them truly joined. Hereafter there may be those who will cry, "Give us of your oil, for our lamps are gone out."

May I not, then, counsel you to "hold fast that which thou hast, that no man take thy crown." Prayer you have proved to be a power, and therefore you must pray. Two revivals, and the addition of over a hundred persons in these three years, demonstate the fact. You have learned with gladness the "more excellent way" of love and close association, therefore, let none divide you—let there be "no schism in the body." "If ye know these things, happy are ye if ye do them."

The conscientiousness, developed by our present system of finance, must not be cast aside. But there will need to be a wiser and more generous liberality on the part of those whom God has blessed with means. The kingdom and house of God should be dear to every worshipper.

But why should I proceed as though you required a charge to do your duty? Surely, the experience of a church which two years hence should celebrate its semi-centennial, must suffice to have established what is the true way of happiness, the truest mode of peace. The same Church-Session, who have kindly and firmly administered the discipline and cared for the doctrine of this church, are at your service. The same Deacons watch over your poor. The same Trustees plan and provide. You have made it a matter of conscience to select them wisely, and I do not fear that they will fail you now.

V. And now it is time for us to part. In harmony and good-will we have lived together, in harmony and good-will we separate. We have rejoiced together with the living, and we have often wept together by the coffin of the dead. Face after face comes out upon the canvas of my thought—each face full of its story. You have made me your friend, your confidant, your counselor. You have come to me sorrowing for sin, and I have heard the first crying of your new-born souls. You have come to me with your burdened hearts, and we have placed the cares of life on "Him who careth for us." You have sought me as your spiritual physician, and I have administered to you the "Balm that is in

Gilead." I have gone after the straying, and helped the hurt, and been happy with the whole.

Whatever may have been the faults of the preaching, the Lord has overruled its "foolishness" to the salvation of souls. I have striven to give you always the best I had, and the lecture-room has been as blessèd as the room above. That desire for knowledge which is so marked a feature of this congregation, and of its Sunday-school and Bible-classes, has been met so far as in me lay. I trust that, hid away within your heart may be here and there a thought which shall recall me to you in the days to come.

Let us be thankful, then, for these years which we have spent together—these Passovers which have celebrated our deliverance "out of the land of Egypt, and out of the house of bondage." We may not forget each other, for we are a part of each others' lives. Yet now

> "I hear a voice you cannot hear,
> Which says I must not stay:
> I see a hand you cannot see,
> Which beckons me away."

In the advancing years, you too, may comprehend that shape of duty which I alone upon my Brocken height can now behold. I hardly hope that you can yet perceive it—nor that you can, see as I see, the clear road of your own future. But, when we are together beyond these mists, within the realm of light, we shall only wonder that we sighed about the nests that were apart, while forest and blue heaven were to be filled and thrilled with song.

Like those last words of warning, of love and of regret, with which we watch our dear ones passing from our side, are these my words to you. It is I who am stationary upon that will of God, which bears me now away. To me, upon my sphere of duty, you are like a known and lovely orb, whose steady planetary movement I shall watch from the rim of my new earth. Better than any one else, I shall interpret your precessions, your retrogressions, and the shifting of your place among the stars. For I know you, like myself, to be lighted by the same Sun of Righteousness, and to hold an unvarying orbit about His throne of truth. I shall test you with the spectroscope; I shall follow you with the telescope. And I shall hear across dim wastes of air your songs of salvation, and the pæans of your joy.

They tell us of a mariner who, contrary to the custom of his class, brought to every new land the best seeds and the choicest plants.

He tended them, and saw to their success—he taught the native islanders to trust him, and to care for what he gave. And then he sailed away, to renew on other shores his benevolent design. And thus he scattered Edens across the summer sea, blessing and being blessed—a true evangelist in the common gifts of God.

And if, to-night, like him, I leave behind me the seeds of truth, and the plants of goodly plans, I know that, like him, I shall be ever welcome back. Like him, I shall linger lovingly, now and then, beside some precious growth, and when I go on board my vessel I shall find her name to be the Good Hope, freighted with generous wishes and fervent prayers, and bound—beyond all transient harbors—for the Port of Everlasting Peace.

UNIVERSITY OF MICHIGAN
3 9015 03581 9500

www.ingramcontent.com/pod-product-compliance
Lightning Source LLC
LaVergne TN
LVHW020634110826
845149LV00004B/1185
9781418190880